GOlden Dreams

some 5 am thoughts

Parth

India | USA | UK

Made with ❤ on the BookLeaf Publishing Platform
www.bookleafpub.in
www.bookleafpub.com

Dedication

Dedication

To the roots that nourish me,
 My parents, whose love shapes the soil of my being.
 Your wisdom, your patience, and your quiet strength
 Are the quiet muses behind these words.

To the readers, who find something of themselves
 In the inked threads of these pages,
 Your hearts are the mirrors where this work finds its
reflection.
 Thank you for your time, your attention, your trust.

To the idea that lives beyond thought,
 To the spark that lights the dark corners of the mind
 And whispers in the stillness —
 You are the silent architect of every poem here.

To Time, the ever-present, ever-fleeting companion,
 For your steady march, which grants us both
 Moments and memories,
 And for showing me how precious it is to be present.

And finally, to Writing —
 This art, this fragile, enduring dance of language,

That allows the soul to breathe,
To wander, to wonder, to feel.
Through you, I find the shape of my thoughts,
The voice of my heart, and the wings of my dreams.

Preface

Acknowledgements

Thanks to Mummy, Papa & Friends.

1.

My mind,

Thinks of the beyond.

Of what lies there.
Of what it feels like,
Of what the fruits there taste,
Of what smell exist,
Of the people.

But it thinks more &
Falls to the chaos of
Reality!

2.

Pregnant with the thoughts of heaven,

A soul wanted to part.

Happy for the fact that it would be
rejoicing in the riches,

Immerse in the beauty
& the fine wine.

Little did it know that,
its time was not over yet.

3.

An angel from heaven came to me,
she was beautiful,
with wings and her halo.
she lured me with her charms.

And took me to the city with huge gates above
the clouds.

I enjoyed my time with her.

Bid her farewell and was on my way back.
The gates opened, but
I did not know the way back.

The Angel came to me & smiled.

She whispered to me,
"just close your eyes and you'll be there"

It was true,
now I miss the Angel.

4.

They say
GOD decides,
who goes to heaven.

And pray to him
that they be allowed.

But you got to
go through the pain
first.
That of Death,
Of leaving everything
And everyone.

And no one ever
prays for that!

5.

To die in valor,
To raise a cup,
To drink with the Gods,
To be a proud fighter,
A legend long remembered,
To have your songs
sung for centuries.

Is to wish for Valhalla.
where the valkyrie take you.
It's a dream.

A dream only few fulfill.

6.

The eternity,
The nothingness,
The liberation
of soul.

We all strive for *'moksha'*

To what extent,
and what can be done for it.

who knows?

7.

The Day of Judgement.
Qayamat
Will decide,
where
The One God
wants you to go.

How balanced are your sins,
the *haram*
with your goods,
the *halal.*

You can attain the Heavens,
Jannat
or
you'll get the Hell,
Jahannum

Choose your deeds wisely.

8.

The steps were
countless,
The rooms were
innumerable.

It was too deep
to measure through
eyes.

It was too painful
for the senses to
even feel.

The beings had horns
& pointed tails.

Yes, it was
Hell.

9.

'To Hell with You'
is often heard
in a conversation,
when there's too
much heat.

Don't you think?
That you're binding
yourself to some
person for going
there.

Be careful
with your words.

10.

The Netherworld,
where the demons rule.

Do they rule fairly?
&
who sets their rules?

Is everyone's voice
heard there?

If it is all true.
Then I would like
to visit.
Someday maybe.

11.

The sky in hell.
Is it Blue?
Does Sun rise in the east?
Does the moon shine at night?
The rivers fluent with water.
The peaks touching horizon.

It seems all alike.

The place is here.
don't look any far.
we're living in it.

12.

'only sinners go to Hell'

'who are we,
but simple beings'

'you'd be judged
per your deeds'

'but we've all sinned
many'

'then prepare for it'.

13.

The god of Death
awaits your presence.

There was a knock on
my door.

I tell him to wait a little.

But the response comes,
'last time you said
it was years back'.

And I get it.
I'm not just ready yet,
my soul with its gates closed
wonders,
when will be ready enough?

14.

I'm tired of all the descending
stairs.
can't I take a lift?

You must finish it by foot.
It's a punishment.

Isn't what lies ahead
the ultimate punishment?

Let me just relax and make the way
swift enough.

Who knows I might not survive it.

15.

The clouds.
blue sky.
oceans,
sun.
The rivers,
moon.
The valleys,
mounts.

Let them all cleanse your soul.

Be at peace with just being.

16.

I fell in love,

With a star,

It was watching over me.
all nights.

We stared at each other.

One night it was gone.

It died,
leaving me a wish to make.

I wished for us to meet again.
Soon.

17. New Poem

The heavy tree,
with leaves &
branches extended.

Spread its bosom,
to shade the
creatures.

The others asked,
'thou art so graceful.
to what end?'

The old one says
'until mother needs'.

18.

A black raven.
Flown.
Flew past my shadow.

I turned to look,
And lo,
My shadow was gone.

It followed the raven,
into the deep dungeons.

I was scared.

The raven now
looked at me.
Its eyes black.
Telling me to be at ease.

'you're here.
enjoy yourself.
the shadow is
what remains.'

19.

Up from the mountains.
A wanderer,
preached to the world.

'be thankful and rejoice'

'the nature has bountiful'

'you just need to live by its
laws'.

20.

The rain.
wash away all your sins.

Falls every season.

Go out &
be soaked.

21.

The moon,
ever so beautiful.

I want to bring
all its light.

Pour it all.

That we may never sleep.

22.

Dear self,
Be proud,
you been good,

But treat
others with care.

For this loop
is great

You support them
and
they do you.

23.

Me,
I am a humble being.

I respect the laws.

I love nature.

I can be you
and you, me.

24.

The parents.
gave birth,
took great care,
shape your future,
loved you
selfless.

Respect and
make them proud.

you'll be one soon.

25.

Brushing through
my body,
went past me.
The blowing winds.
Am I too hollow?
does my existence
mean not
to them.

'No one's too full.
to contain us'

They just keep blowing.

26.

My self.
my pride.
my being.

Means everything to me.

Then I look at the
world,
from above.

And there..

all my feelings melt.

27.

I looked at you.

I saw you smile,
or maybe it was your soul.

I smile back but you didn't notice,
that goes for me too.

I embraced you and we were one.

But I stood here and you there.

28.

With clothes on.
the body comforts.

With the body.
the spirit does.

With no bounds,
it rises above
and flies off.

29.

A paper,
turned to value.

A soul,
turned to name.

A star,
called to an object.

What then is
Real?

Here is
The Universe.

30.

A city that was,
to be hated.

Turned out to
be a city
long remembered
and missed.

It was a wonderful
journey,
Which I despised and
loved at the same
time.

31.

Why do you build
walls around
your heart?

Let the love flow.

Haven't you heard,
'what goes around,
comes around.'

32.

Building a castle
at the shore
only to look at
it and wait
for it to be
swept away.

What are the cities?
the roads?
the buildings?
the houses?
That we built,
but castles to be swept away.

One day.

You must see.

33.

When you feel pain,
you put it to words.

The pain is here to stay,
it has as job to do.

But you would have
just invented your poetry.

34.

Defeat,
It is so personal.

There was a moment
when everyone wants
to succumb.

Then you're done with it.
You horn it and
power from the hurt.

Defeat,
Is a lovely thing.

You want to make it your last
and hope to win.
it teaches you more ways to conquer.

Defeat,
Eventually surrenders
to you.

You the master,
Hold it dear.

35.

Falling to reason,
with the reasoning.

What shall that culminate to be.

The reason is always a longing.

the reasoning always an eye opener,
the logic.

Who shall I side with?

maybe I'll take the reason.

36.

In this reality.

Where I float.
and birds crawl.

Where you are always holding me.
mine.

I must go mad.

But can't even dare to accept it.

37.

How can I measure time,
the endless.

Is it meridiem,
the ante & post.

Is it by the sun & moon.

Or by summer & winter.

I don't know.
if it goes straight,
or has branches.

Does it stay as
past, present and future.
or the other way around.

Till then I guess
my time would have come.

38.

Home sweet home.

We fight over is it yours or mine.
who put the first brick.
who brought up the idea.

Where is it located.
close to our hearts.
place where our bodies rest.
after a tiresome day.

Where our babies giggle,
where our feet tingle.
our souls cuddle.
Home sweet home.

39.

A wonderful song,
written by me.

The chorus was
always pain.

The verses were a
great melody of my
success.

The beats
my pleasures.

It ends only in
5 minutes.

How short a story to tell.

40.

The pain always teaches
you lessons.
Lessons that no teacher
ever can.

It teaches us to live.

To embrace every thing
that we hold dear and
be content.

It also lets you know the
right faces of people.

What a wonderful thing.
Pain.

41.

What is pleasure?
But pain incarnate,
if you will.

What can it give you,
but a small joy.

Be watchful maybe
the gods won't like it.

42.

Burning fire.
By which they sat,
to warm themselves
in the freezing cold.

Burning fire,
That helped them
cook for the two meals
they hardly managed.

The fire,
That gave light to
them in the dark nights.

The fire,
finally consumed them.

43.

I'm taken aback,
to the memories of
past.
where I climbed the mountain.
Reached the peak,
screamed till I was content.
Held your hands.
Kissed you,
and sat there with
arms around your waist.

Before I know.
It's getting dark
and time to Descend.

44.

Do you fear?

I obviously do.
Of the light that
it might blind me.
Of the heat that
it might kill me.

Of getting pulled back
in the past life,
or if my coffee gets cold.

Conquer!
You live in the present.

45.

They anointed my forehead,
before I went to war.

They did again,
for an auspicious union.

And finally,
To prepare for death.

But the smell that it
gave was always in
my heart of,
Victory.

46.

Attaching
and
Detaching

two words,
worlds apart.
but pretty much
sum up
the life of a
human.

Ever thought about that?

47.

The moon changes
from full to none.

The sun falls to the
eclipse.

The stars die of their
own volition.

What do you think is
permanent?

Your life!

48.

From a bud
emerged a lily.
so pretty.
I loved it,
it smelled great.
was a pleasure to my eyes,
my senses.

Too tempted,
I decided to pluck
it out and place it
on my desk.

It dies.

49.

A murderer.
I kill,
myself.

In many ways.
All the time.
in my mind.

50.

Like slaves,
You & I,
survive this cruelty.
That the world has
forced on us.

The struggle is real
and it is called,
living.

51.

Do we kneel to the God.
or do we bow to the power that he has.

Yes, we have seen what power does,
it plays with minds and can even be dangerous.

What is the question here.
Do you feel that you've got the power.
for you to challenge her for a duel.
The winner takes all, obviously.

To question the existence of you.
That is me, him, her, they.
for all's sake.

Go out riding on your stallion.
wielding your sword,
clad with the armor.
may there be a halo over your head.
and a flag in your hand that has you message on it.

The flag is plain White.

52.

A hand writes,
to the mind's will,
and the heart's content,
that is the invention of poetry.

53.

A cup of tea,
smelling so great.
It soothes my soul.

Or is it the feeling of me
going to take a sip,
A sip of wine
from heaven, taken on the
auspices of earth.

Who am I but a fool.
I devour my cup full.
and still want more.
The cup of tea,
it is.
Chamomile.

54.

Shed your skin,
to be reborn.
A snake does
and it completely changes.

why don't we,
we must learn to.
At some point we
have to shed the skin.

To adjust,
To cope with this
world full of disguises.

55.

Hold your heart,
dear.

No one deserves
its love,
more than
You.

56.

Yesterday I was the glowing
bright sun.

Today the beautiful
moon.

Tomorrow the radiating
star.

The day after,
may be the sky.

I've never been myself enough.

57.

The glass to my window broke,

I came home and
the gushing breeze
chilled me to the core.

I guess the wind broke it,

But alas,
I found a letter attached with
a stone.

It read,
I'm breaking it,
enjoy yourself.

It was my heart,
to mend,
which I always do.

I put the stone
in cold storage
of the Heap.

58.

My dear diary,
I make entries daily,
I never lie to you,
You're my respite.
you complete me,
My confidant.

Dear diary,
so small.
Yet so full of life.
So silent,
Yet fluent with
emotions.
My Diary.
You just be never ending.

59.

Who are you.

I see you everyday,
in the mirror.
You always smile at me.
You even look like me.

Do I know you?

60.

'are you Man enough,
to take everything?'
They say all the time.

But what do they expect of men.
are we not but living creatures.
with hunger and fire
and emotions in us.
Do we not want to weep
our loss and
be joyful in our
triumphs.

Are we not man enough already.

61.

What is the legacy
that you've built.

I've written it for my
ancestors to be remembered by.

I've written it for my
descendants to be proud of.

But I've lived enough to
satisfy my contemporaries.

62.

All we do work,
for our lives.

Some for luxury,
some to just live by.

To fill the void in one's life.
or
to find a means.

I don't know what it means
to work
& why get paid.

63.

To Understand my thoughts,

I had a meeting with my mind.

It told me to consult the heart.

I talked to him over a coffee.
to get the response,

'your thoughts are the reflection of yourself'.

64.

Remember,

Who you're
doing it for.

65.

To cry by my side,

I need a friend,

Who hits me till
I've finished up.
with all my might,
and emptied.

66.

How did a person
come here?

surely his mother bore him,
maybe there was an idea of him.
maybe it was a mistake.
Or
Maybe he was called upon
by someone.

How would I know,
I'm just one of the person.

67.

67

Sinks below the skin,
piercing through the heart,
The beauty of her.

To keep us alive.

68.

My stomach hurts,
from the food of last night.

I ate your love,
but it shouldn't,
I should be blessed,
I don't want to throw it out,
So I hold that ache
and find a way to
reduce the pan.

69.

Agitated I throw my pen
at the sky.
The ink colors
cloud black.
its darkening.
I'm struck by thunder.
I die.

70.

Looking at the sky,

Cherish the beauty
of the creation.
that God has done.

71.

Love thyself.

No one else,
No one.
can do so.

72.

Be proud,
You've lived
this far.

73.

The essence of love,
of life,
is the food for soul.

It nourishes,
it feeds,
to see it bloom
and spread its udders,
to suckle.

It perishes,
to leave you
dead.

74.

Stand up to your
calling.

Don't close your eyes to it.

It may not come again.

Rise.

75.

Aloneness,
by being myself.
I dig deep and
peep into the subconscious.
it makes me feel blessed.

Then comes the
loneliness,
with people around.
I feel left out,
aloneness forced
that is a crime.

76.

All is well
that ends
well.

But the end
still eludes
keeps hope high.

No one's ever
ready and it
still arrives
the wicked end.

It has to be
well.

77.

With love
from me.

I seek
thy love.

Will meet again
in our tryst.

9 789369 530540